Speaking and Listening

Kate Ruttle

CONTENTS

HOW TO USE MIND'S EYE SPEAKING and LISTENING

'Communication is crucial.'

'The ability to communicate is an essential life skill for all children and young people in the twenty-first century. It is at the core of all social interaction. With effective communication skills, children can engage and thrive. Without them, children will struggle to learn, achieve, make friends and interact with the world around them.'

These words are taken from the latest report on the Speech, Language and Communication needs of children and young people from 0-19 years. (The Bercow Report DCSF-00632-2008).

The Mind's Eye speaking and listening packs offer teachers exciting and engaging ways to develop the speaking and listening skills necessary for life and learning. As a parent of a five year old child said in the report: *"Speech, language and communication is the most important thing in all our children ... It's their key to life"*

There are three different kinds of speaking and listening activity in this pack. They are defined by the initial stimulus offered.

- Images (units 1 – 20). For these units, the starting point for the class discussion is a photograph.
- Sounds (units 21 – 25). For these units, the starting point is a brief audio clip.
- Scripted activities (units 26 – 30). For these units, the initial part of the activity involves the children listening to instructions on the CD and following them on the worksheet.

Teaching a unit

Follow the step-by-step instructions at the top of the Teacher's Notes page. This will help to stimulate and build on prior knowledge and provide a context for the following activities. All of the units follow the same progression:

- start by exploring the stimulus closely, following the suggestions in the grey panel on the teacher's page.

Thereafter, you can choose to work through an additional sequence of activities involving

- speaking
- listening
- drama
- group work.

You can either follow the sequence described on the page, or simply select one of the activities to focus on.

All of the units are linked to aspects of the Year 2 curriculum. See page 64 for details.

PRIMARY NATIONAL STRATEGY FRAMEWORK FOR LITERACY
www.standards.dcsf.gov.uk/primaryframework/literacy

TEACHING OBJECTIVES COVERED IN MIND'S EYE YEAR 2

SPEAKING	• Speak with clarity and use appropriate intonation when reading and reciting texts • Tell real and imagined stories using the conventions of familiar story language • Explain ideas and processes using imaginative and adventurous vocabulary and non-verbal gestures to support communication
LISTENING	• Listen to others in class, ask relevant questions and follow instructions • Listen to talk by an adult, remember some specific points and identify what they have learned • Respond to presentations by describing characters, repeating some highlights and commenting constructively
GROUP DISCUSSION	• Ensure that everyone contributes, allocate tasks, and consider alternatives and reach agreement • Work effectively in groups by ensuring that each group member takes a turn challenging, supporting and moving on • Listen to each other's views and preferences, agree the next steps to take and identify contributions by each group member
DRAMA	• Adopt appropriate roles in small or large groups and consider alternative courses of action • Present part of traditional stories, their own stories or work drawn from different parts of the curriculum for members of their own class • Consider how mood and atmosphere are created in live or recorded performance

MAKING PROGRESS IN SPEAKING and LISTENING

In the handbook *Speaking, Listening, Learning: working with children in Key Stages 1 and 2,* the DfES (2003) sets objectives for children to achieve in each key stage. The activities in Mind's Eye Year 1 all make progress towards the Key Stage 1 objectives, which are:

Speaking: Children at the end of Year 2 should be able to speak clearly and expressively in supportive contexts where the topic is familiar, or there is a pattern to follow in stories they have heard or read. When recounting events or actions, children's talk should be reasonably ordered and well paced. Their talk should be engaging to listeners through the use of emphasis and varied intonation, and they should also be able to use gestures and visual aids to highlight meanings.

Listening: Children at the end of Year 2 should be able to listen actively in a context where there are practical consequences to following what the speakers say. They should have explicit understanding of some of the ways listening may be demonstrated, such as the need to look at the person speaking and ask them to repeat anything not understood. They should also be able to clarify and retain what they have heard, not only by trying to act on instructions but also by rephrasing in collaboration with others and then asking 'the experts' for more specific information.

Group discussion: Children at the end of Year 2 should be able to participate in group work of different kinds, understanding how to use talk purposefully in pairs and small groups, and to contribute ideas in plenary and whole-class discussions. When working in groups, they should be able to make and share predictions, take turns, and note results that feed into an account of what they have done. Year 2 children should also have some understanding of how to comment on the effectiveness of group discussions, taking account of the topics talked about and how some particular uses of language help to communicate ideas.

Drama: Children at the end of Year 2 should be able to develop work in role where contexts are provided, either through discussion or from shared reading. They should be able to create characters imaginatively, making effective use of space and gestures, and talk about different characters' actions and feelings. In responding to performances they are able to say what they enjoyed or liked about what they have seen and heard.

ASSESSING AND RECORDING

To be able to trace pupils' progress effectively, follow these guidelines:

Make notes: much of the pupils' learning in speaking and listening takes place spontaneously, as comments are exchanged and ideas shared within paired and group discussions. Keep a 'talk diary' in which you can record notable comments made by pupils in the course of a Mind's Eye activity.

Take digital photographs: whenever possible, take digital photos of specific children involved in Mind's Eye activities to include in a class 'Speaking and Listening Learning Journey' record book. Allow children to share this book with friends as another source for talk.

Set goals: prior to a Mind's Eye activity, select specific targets drawn from the 'Making Progress' sections above and express them to the children, e.g. ' This time, look at the person you're speaking to.'

Encourage self-evaluation: encourage the children to reflect upon their own progress in speaking and listening by evaluating their own progress in Mind's Eye activities using a simple pictorial record sheet e.g. smiley faces, traffic lights.

Share successes: at the end of a particularly effective session, share ideas and elicit the children's own views about how they contributed and why the session was successful.

Record performances: using video cameras and/or audio equipment, record discussions and oral presentations. Play back and evaluate together.

Arrange 'assessed' activities: choose a specific Mind's Eye activity and explain to the class that it will be used as an assessment so they understand that for this particular activity you will be scoring the contributions made by each pupil. Plan to cover one activity from Speaking, Listening, Group Discussion and Drama over the course of the book (taken from a variety of different units).

Unit 1/TELL ME A STORY

TEACHER'S NOTES

Introduction

- Load up the Mind's Eye CD-ROM. You may like to tell the children what the title of the session is before you reveal the image, or just open up the picture.

- With the image in view, ask the children for their first impressions. What does the photo show? Do you think the puppets are doing a show? Why? What kind of puppets are these?

Familiarisation

- What kinds of puppets have children got at home? String, hand, finger, shadow? Talk about how different kinds of puppets work.

- Have they ever used puppets? What for?

Exploration

- Which different characters can they see? What is the evidence?

- Look at the puppets' clothes. What can we find out about how they were made? Discuss the fact that the clothes are not painted on, but carefully made. Why would someone bother to do that?

- Are these puppets made for children, adults or the whole family? How do we know?

Souvenir puppets from Prague Old Town.
© Danita Delimont/Alamy

ACTIVITIES

Speaking

- **Creating a story:** Look at the photograph again. Ask children to decide who they think the hero of the story in the puppet show. Is there a villain? Is it one of the puppets, or are there other puppets we can't see that include a villain? Work together to create the outline of a story involving all of these characters and perhaps one or two others. Don't invent the ending though.

- **Telling a story:** Let the children work with a partner to tell the whole story of the puppet show, including the ending. Once all children have finished, swap the pairs around so that children tell their stories to a new partner.

Listening

- **Hot-seating:** Choose one of the characters from the puppet show and choose someone to be hot-seated as the character in the image. (If children haven't experienced hot-seating before, you or another adult will need to model how to be the hot-seated character.) Remind children of the *wh-* question words (*who, why, when, where, which*) and how. Let the children ask *wh-* questions of that character to find out more about them. Encourage children to think about previous answers before they frame their next question.

Group work

- **Creating a new puppet:** Talk about how you would set about creating some kind of a dragon puppet to accompany the puppets on the photograph. Ask each group to decide what they want to make, the materials they need and the process by which they would make their puppet. Let them use paper to record their instructions. Each group can send an envoy to a different group to explain the instructions and see if the new group can suggest improvements.

Drama

- **Mime:** Choose one of the stories that the children created around the characters. First, ask the children each to choose a character from their story. Explore the characterisation of their characters. *How would they walk, sit down or eat? What kind of sports would they play? How would they get dressed in the morning?* Let children explore their own responses to the questions through mime and role play and work in groups to develop a mime to tell their story.

Writing activity

- Children can use their PCM to write their story. Remind them to include details to improve the characterisation. Alternatively, children could make a display poster showing how to create their puppet.

Name _____ Date _____

PUPPET SHOW

Write your puppet story here.

_____

_____

_____

_____

_____

_____

_____

_____

_____

_____

_____

_____

_____

_____

_____

_____

Mind's Eye Y2/Speaking & Listening   Unit 1/TELL ME A STORY

TEACHER'S NOTES

Introduction

- Load up the Mind's Eye CD-ROM. You may like to tell the children what the title of the session is before you reveal the image, or just open up the picture.

- With the image in view, ask the children for their first impressions. What does the photo show? Is this natural or made by someone? How do you know?

Familiarisation

- Introduce the work of Andy Goldsworthy. He's an artist who uses nature for the materials and inspiration for his work. He's very interested in how light and colour can make a work of art even more beautiful. This work is in Scotland.

Exploration

- Ask the children to look more closely at the image, as if they are detectives, and find out all that they can about it, including the materials Goldsworthy has used. Why aren't all the stones the same colour? Why did he use rough stones, not smooth stones? Ask the children if they think he found the stones near where he built the sculpture, or whether they think he brought them with him on lorries. Ask them to explain their answers.

- Talk about where the sculpture is built. Why might Goldsworthy have decided to build it on top of a hill? Would he have built this same sculpture in the middle of a city?

- Ask the children for their responses to the sculpture as a work of art.

Andy Goldsworthy sculpture, Penpont, Dumfries and Galloway, Scotland. © *Gary Cook/Alamy*

ACTIVITIES

Speaking

- **Building a scene:** Look at the photograph again. What was the weather like when the photograph was taken? What would it feel like, up on the hill, near the sculpture at this time?

- Ask the children to close their eyes and imagine what it would be like on top of that hill in a howling gale and a driving wind. Can they give you words to describe both the sculpture and what it would be like to be near it? Now imagine the same scene, but on a baking hot day with only a slight breeze. How would it have changed?

Listening

- **Building a sound scene:** Look at the photograph again. What kinds of noises might there be up on the hill top in different weathers and at different times of day? Might there be any sounds from the weather, such as wind, rain, thunder, lightning? Could there be any sound from animals, birds or aeroplanes? Would there be traffic sounds or sounds of people? How would the sounds change at night? Discuss all the sounds the children can think of which you might hear by that statue in the course of a year.

Group work

- **Soundscape:** Let children work in groups to create a sound scene. They should decide which weather and time of day they want to represent, then find ways of creating appropriate sounds. Let the groups perform their sound scenes to each other. Can a different group work out which time of day and weather the sound scene is creating?

Drama

- **Planning:** Let the children work in groups to discuss how they think the sculpture was built. How did the stones get to where they are? How many people built the sculpture? Did they work from a design, or did it evolve?

- **Mime:** In their groups, let the children mime all the stages in the building of the sculpture. They will need to assign roles within the group.

Writing activity

- Write two paragraphs about the sculpture and then ask the children to think about how they would design their own nature sculpture. Draw it on the PCM.

Name _____ Date _____

ART OUTSIDE

Andy Goldsworthy's sculpture

Description

_____

_____

_____

Setting

_____

_____

My nature sculpture

I would use _____

This is what my sculpture would look like.

TEACHER'S NOTES

Introduction

• Load up the Mind's Eye CD-ROM. You may like to tell the children what the title of the session is before you reveal the image, or just open up the picture.

• With the image in view, ask the children for their first impressions. What does the photo show? What are these buildings built for? How do we know?

Familiarisation

• Tell the children that this is a picture of the Swiss Re Lloyds Insurance Building in London. The architect is Sir Norman Foster.

Exploration

• Ask the children to look more closely at the image, as if they are detectives, and find out all that they can about it, including discussing the possible function of the cranes (why are they blue?), and of the metal pipes coming from the building in the foreground.

• Look at the shape of the tallest building. It's often known as 'the Gherkin'. Explain what gherkins are and what they look like and ask children to decide whether they think it's a fair name for the building. Can they suggest a better one?

'The Gherkin', Swiss Re Lloyds Insurance Building, London.
© PCL/Alamy

ACTIVITIES

Group work

• **Focused viewing:** Look at the photograph again, but this time ask different groups of children to consider different aspects of the buildings. One group can focus on, for example, the overall shape of the buildings, the shape of the windows and decoration on the surfaces of the buildings, another focuses on the materials that the building is made of and the functionality of its different parts. Within their groups, different children should take responsibility for sketching, writing and describing the picture, explaining their findings to the rest of the class.

Listening

• **Feedback:** After each group has fed back on their observations, ask other groups to collaborate to develop questions about the building. Don't let individual children ask questions until they have been agreed in the group first. Model asking questions that build upon what has already been said and encourage the children to do the same.

Speaking

• **Evaluation:** Once children have completed the group work activity, spend some time evaluating the experience. How did ideas develop? Were one person's ideas always accepted, or were they discussed and built upon? Did everyone contribute ideas? How could each group have worked more effectively?

Drama

• **Working life:** Revisit discussions you have had about the purposes of the buildings as office space. Take the children with you on a virtual visit to a huge modern office block like the one in the picture. Create for them the cathedral-like size of the atrium. How do you behave in there? How do you speak? Cram in a lift together and move out to explore one of the floors. What are people doing? How are they moving and talking?

Writing activity

• Ask the children to design their own building inspired by an everyday food item. They should use the PCM and add captions and a title to their design. They need to think about the purpose and function of the building. Is it a house, workplace, factory, shop or restaurant? Where will it be built? Is it in a city, on a hill or in the countryside? Is it going to be built from specific materials? What colour(s) will it be?

Name _____ Date _____

A FOOD BUILDING ? ? ? ? ? ?

Choose a type of food, and thinking about its shape and features, draw your design for a building based on your food idea – just like The Gherkin! Add labels to explain your picture.

My food building is based on _____

TEACHER'S NOTES

Introduction

- Load up the Mind's Eye CD-ROM. You may like to tell the children what the title of the session is before you reveal the image, or just open up the picture.

- With the image in view, ask the children for their first impressions. What does the photo show? What kind of car is it? Where is the picture likely to have been taken?

Familiarisation

- This is photograph of Michael Schumacher during the first laps of a Formula 1 race.

- Do the children know what Formula 1 is? Have any of them ever seen it on TV? If so, invite those who have to describe what they saw.

Exploration

- Ask the children to look more closely at the image, as if they are detectives, and find out all that they can about it. How is this car different from cars you see on the roads in towns and cities? What makes it different? Why does it need to be different?

- How is the car the same as cars you see on the roads? What are the features that most cars have in common? Check that the children have the vocabulary to describe the different parts of the car, e.g. *wheels, chassis, body*.

Michael Schumacher driving the Ferrari 248 F1 in 2006.
© *CrashPA/Alamy*

ACTIVITIES

Speaking

- **Explaining:** Look at the photograph again and ask the children questions about this car and other vehicles: *Why do vehicles have wheels? Do they all have the same number and size of wheels? Why are vehicles different shapes? Which parts of vehicles move, light up or make a noise?* As children speak, scaffold the language and structure of explanations so that they understand how they are structured.

Listening

- **Building a sound scene:** Look at the photograph again. What kinds of noises would you hear on a racetrack such as this? Would the noises be loud or soft? Would they be coming from the engines, the wheels, the brakes, the crowd, the TV commentators, the hotdog sellers? Are the noises always exactly the same or do they vary? How do they vary?

Group work

- **Performing the sound scene:** Let children work in groups to create a sound scene of a racetrack. It can be the Grand Prix, any other vehicle race, a horse race, the marathon, school sports day or just a race in the playground. They should decide on one theme to create their sound effects – and bear in mind the noise restrictions of working in a school.

 Drama

- **Planning:** What does it feel like to be a spectator at a race? When is the race most exciting? How do you react when your favourite is leading? Or catching up with the leader? Or near the back of the field? Wins? Comes second? Loses?

- Ask children to work in groups. The group as a whole should decide what kind of race they are going to be watching, how many competitors there are and who will win. The children can then act out the race as spectators. Through their faces, their body language and what they say we should be able to see how the race is progressing.

Writing activity

- Using the PCM, compare a normal car and a Formula 1 racing car. Start by designing a racing car and then list the similarities and differences between this and a standard road car.

Name _____ Date _____

READY, SET, GO!

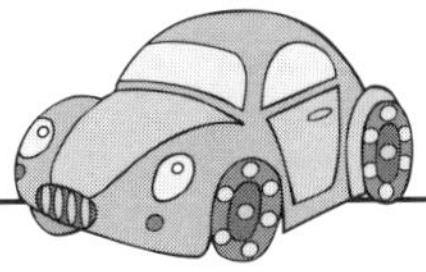

Design your own amazing racing car in the box.

Now list the things about your racing car that are different
from a normal car.

Racing Car   **Normal Car**

_____   _____

_____   _____

_____   _____

_____   _____

TEACHER'S NOTES

Introduction

- Load up the Mind's Eye CD-ROM. You may like to tell the children what the title of the session is before you reveal the image, or just open up the picture.

- With the image in view, ask the children for their first impressions. What does the photo show? What is happening? When was the photo taken?

Familiarisation

- This photograph was taken in Germany in 1971. It was taken during a football game between RW Oberhausen and Bayern Munich.

- Ask one of the children to describe what is happening in this photograph.

Exploration

- Ask the children to look more closely at the image, as if they are detectives, and find out all that they can about it. Is this going to be a goal? Which of the players has just scored the goal? How do you know? Why are some of the players standing and walking, not running around? Did many people want to watch this game? How can we tell? Is the football kit the same as strips today? Describe the similarities and differences.

Football match between Bayern Munich and RW Oberhausen, 1971. © *Werner Otto/Alamy*

ACTIVITIES

 ### Drama

- **Freeze-frame:** Let children work in pairs or threes. Each child in the group should choose a different character that they can see on the screen: the goalie, the goal scorer, one of the other players, a spectator. The children can make a freeze-frame of the shot in the photo (the goalie can stand on the ground!) and then tell each other how they feel. They should describe both emotions and the physical feelings in their bodies. Let the groups perform their freeze-frame to each other.

 ### Speaking

- **Create a story:** Work together to create the story around this picture. Give the characters names and discuss how the build-up to the game might have been. When in the game – in your story – was this goal? Is it the first, the decider, a goal in the middle of the game? Was this goal scored by the winning team, or was it a desperate attempt to catch up? How did the game end? How did the story end?

 ### Group work

- **Telling a story:** Let the children develop the story in pairs, then they can team up with another pair and can tell their stories to each other.

 ### Listening

- **Summarising a story:** After the children have listened to each others' stories, ask the listening pair to retell – in summary form if they can – the story they have just listened to. Both teams can then evaluate the others' performance.

 ## Writing activity

- Children can write the story they have created as a comic strip or storyboard, using the PCM framework. They can use speech bubbles or captions and should shape their story with a beginning, a build-up, an exciting part and a good ending.

FOOTBALL TALES

Write your football tale as a comic strip in the four boxes.
You can use speech bubbles or write underneath each picture to
explain what is going on.

TEACHER'S NOTES

Introduction

- Load up the Mind's Eye CD-ROM. You may like to tell the children what the title of the session is before you reveal the image, or just open up the picture.

- With the image in view, ask the children for their first impressions. Where is the photo taken? What time of year is it? What is the boy doing?

Familiarisation

- Have any of the children ever been to the seaside? Invite them to share their experiences.

Exploration

- Ask the children to look more closely at the image, as if they are detectives, and find out all that they can about it. Is the boy alone at the seaside? They should look carefully at the footprints before they answer the

question. Is it sunny? (Look at the shadows. Do the children know what time of day it is by the length of the shadow?) Is the sea rough or smooth?

Boy on seashore. © *Photographer's Choice/Getty Images*

ACTIVITIES

Speaking

- **Imagining a story:** The children should work in pairs to create a story around the boy. What is he doing at the seaside? What is he thinking? Is he enjoying memories? Planning tomorrow? Looking at a ship? Saying goodbye to the sea because he's going home? Who is his family? Where are they? Is he with his brothers and sisters or friends, or is he alone?

- **Telling a story:** Let the children swap partners. They can then tell their stories to their new partner. Remind the children to speak clearly and try to sequence the events in their story carefully.

 Listening

- **Hot-seating:** Remind children of the *wh-* question words (*who, why, when, where, which*) and how. Choose someone to be hot-seated as the character in the image. (If children haven't experienced hot-seating before, you or another adult will need to model how to be the hot-seated character.) Let the children ask *wh-* questions of that character to find out more about them. Encourage children to think about previous answers before they frame their next question.

Group work

- **Class discussion:** Keep the image on the board as you work. The children should stand with their eyes closed, imagining what they could feel if they were the boy. Think about the sensations of: sand beneath the feet; sun on the skin; incoming waves on the toes. Agree words to describe both the sensations and the emotions they evoke.

- Discuss the sounds you would hear at the seaside including the sound of the waves, seagulls calling, people on the beach, traffic nearby, dogs or horses, and the wind flapping windbreaks or kites.

- **Paired conversations:** Working in pairs or small groups revisit the sounds you might hear at the seaside. Now create a 'soundscape' of a seaside with different children taking different roles and making appropriate noises.

Drama

- **Sensations:** Ask the class to stand in a circle, preferably barefooted. Talk to create a shared role-play image of the seaside, using ideas from children's own experiences. Imagine the sun on your face, the wind in your hair, the feel of the sand underfoot (wriggle your toes all together to see if you can feel it). Dip a toe into the water. Is it warm? Cold? What do you do? Imagine the tide coming in and going out. Share memories of the day that's just finishing at the seaside. What did you do all day? Have a picnic? Build sandcastles? Play in the water? Let the children role play their shared ideas.

Writing activity

- Children could write up any of the stories or accounts they have made doing these activities, including using the PCM. The more of the activities you have done, the richer the language you should expect of the children. Remind them to include the sights, sounds and feelings of the seaside in their writing.

A DAY AT THE SEASIDE

What is the boy thinking about?

Write or draw your ideas in the thought bubbles.

TEACHER'S NOTES

Introduction

• Load up the Mind's Eye CD-ROM. You may like to tell the children what the title of the session is before you reveal the image, or just open up the picture.

• With the image in view, ask the children for their first impressions. What does the photograph show? Where are the children? Is the photograph new or old?

Familiarisation

• Have any of the children ever been to the seaside? Invite them to share their experiences.

• This photograph was taken in Whitby, Yorkshire in 1888. Have any of the class been to Whitby?

Exploration

• Ask the children to look more closely at the image, as if they are detectives, and find out all that they can about it. How do we know that this photograph is not new?

Discuss the sepia colouring of the photograph as well as the children's clothes. What are they wearing? How are their clothes different from clothes we would wear at the seaside today? What is the same about their clothes?

• Is it a nice day in the picture? What evidence is there? Look at the shadows and the light on the sea to establish that it was at least sunny.

Two children pose on Whitby beach, circa 1888.
© POPPERFOTO/Alamy

ACTIVITIES

Speaking

• **Exploration:** Why do people go to the seaside? List as many reasons as you can, for example: holidays, a day out, to walk the dog, to ride their horses, to sell ice-cream or drinks, to watch birds and sea mammals, to go out in a boat, for fishing or crabbing, to find shells, to fly kites, to swim…

• Why would people have gone to the seaside in the past? Look at the photograph and discuss why these girls might have gone. Is it for the same reasons, or different ones to those listed above?

• Discuss how the people on the beach would have looked in Victorian times. Talk about transport to the beach, bathing huts, bathing costumes, what the people on the shore might have worn, talked about, eaten…

Listening

• **I went to the seaside and I took…:** Go round the class asking each person to say one thing that they would take to the seaside. As each child says their item, they should also list all those already mentioned by others.

Group work

• **Same and different:** In their groups, the children should look at the photograph and list everything that is the same about the seaside today and then everything that is different.

• Monitor the groups to check that they all know what their role is and that everyone is being given the opportunity to participate.

Drama

• **Freeze-frame:** The children can work in pairs. Each pair should take up the poses of one of the children in the picture, then develop their own role play from that point. What did the children do after they had posed for the photographer? Did they hold those positions for long, or did they move to become more comfortable? Did they return to their mother or go for a paddle? Perhaps they build sandcastles – but what about their clothes? Complete the scenario.

Writing activity

• Write a poem about a day at the seaside either in modern times or in the past. The children can write about themselves or the girls in the photograph. Use the ideas from the activities to develop ideas for the poem or let the children discuss holidays that their parents or grandparents have taken.

Name _____   Date _____

SEASIDE POEM

Write a seaside poem. You can use the picture to give you ideas or write about a day out with your own family and friends.

TEACHER'S NOTES

Introduction

- Load up the Mind's Eye CD-ROM. You may like to tell the children what the title of the session is before you reveal the image, or just open up the picture.

- With the image in view, ask the children for their first impressions. What does the photograph show? What kind of settlement are we looking at? What are the clues?

Familiarisation

- This is a photograph of the village of Arinagour, the only village on the Isle of Coll in the Western Isles of Scotland.

- Children who have read the Katie Morag books may know that they are based on Coll, where the author lives, so this is the village that Katie Morag must live in.

Exploration

- Ask the children to look more closely at the image, as if they are detectives. What is the evidence that this is an island? How would a fishing village on the coast look different? Why are there so many boats all grouped together? How did the cars get to the island? How do all the clothes and food for the people get to the island?

Cottages in Arinagour, the only village on Coll, Western Isles, Scotland, and home to half of the est. 180 population.
© *John Warburton-Lee/Alamy*

ACTIVITIES

Speaking

- **Discussion:** Look at the photograph and talk about how Arinagour is the same as and different to the place where you live. Discuss what the people who live on the island might do. Think about the kinds of shops there might be (a post office and general stores and a tourist shop that sells local crafts), how the land is used for farming sheep, why people might open hotels or bed and breakfasts. There is at least one author/illustrator, as well as other artists and other craftspeople. Do the children go to school? (Yes!) What other work might people do? (Minister, tractor drivers, bus driver, postman, milkman, ferrymen, fishermen.)

Group work

- **Lucky or unlucky?:** In their groups, the children should consider whether children who live on Coll are lucky or unlucky. They should list all the advantages and disadvantages of island living and come to a group decision. Each group should send an envoy to another group to give their group's decision and explain their reasoning.

Listening

- **Asking questions:** Let the envoy from two of the groups (ideally with opposing opinions) explain their groups' reasoning to the class. Ask the other children to listen to the reasoning and ask questions to tease out the ideas. Model question types that challenge, without being too aggressive or assertive.

Drama

- **Handshakes:** Let each of the children choose a character who might live on Coll. They should decide for themselves what their name is, what their occupation is, whether they like it or not and whether they like island living.

- Ask all the children to walk around the hall until you clap your hands, then they should find someone nearby, shake their hand and start a conversation as if with a stranger.

Writing activity

- Ask the children to write down three things that you think would be good fun about living on an island, based on the group discussions and the photograph. Remind the children to use headings in their writing. Encourage them to think about the lives of the island's children and compare them with their own lives. They should think about school, hobbies, places to see on outings, food, housing, etc. They could also write three bad things as an extension activity if time permits.

Name _____ Date _____

ISLAND LIVING

Write about three things you think would be great about living on an island. Give each paragraph its own heading. You can draw a picture for each one too!

1 _____

_____

_____

_____

_____

2 _____

_____

_____

_____

_____

3 _____

_____

_____

_____

_____

Unit 9/SPORT OF KINGS

TEACHER'S NOTES

Introduction

- Load up the Mind's Eye CD-ROM. You may like to tell the children what the title of the session is before you reveal the image, or just open up the picture.

- With the image in view, ask the children for their first impressions. What do they think this picture shows? What do they think the men are doing?

Familiarisation

- Do children know why horse racing is called the Sport of Kings? Three Kings, James I, his son Charles I, and his son Charles II all enjoyed horse racing at Newmarket and it was during this time that the rules and traditions of horse racing became established.

- Have any of the children ever been horse racing or seen it on TV? If so, ask them to explain what happens to the rest of the class.

- Link the historical period in which this picture was painted (early 1700s) with the Great Fire of London. Writing diaries was one way of recording the events of the day; painting pictures was another. This was before the invention of photographs and films.

Exploration

- Look at the picture together and try to find as much information as possible about the race. How many people are racing? Which horse is winning? Why are some men sitting on horseback but not racing?

- Look at the people who aren't on horseback. What are they doing?

- Look carefully at the horses' legs. This picture was painted before people began to understand that horses didn't run like dogs. No horse ever runs with both front legs stretched out at the same time.

Racing at Newmarket, John Wooton. Private collection
© *Ackermann and Johnson Ltd., London/The Bridgeman Art Library*

ACTIVITIES

Speaking

- **Sports day:** Most children will have experienced a sports day in school. If they don't do competitive sports, focus their attention on some other occasion when they – or their team – might win or lose, e.g. team games in PE, football, playground races, board games, party games. Talk about their experiences of winning and losing.

- Ask them to think about what it means to be a winner. How do you feel? What can you do to show people how you feel? Can you help those who didn't win to feel better? How does it feel when someone else wins? What do you do to show your feelings? How do you feel about the winner?

Listening

- **Sounds of racing:** Let children work in groups to look carefully at the pictures again. What kind of sounds do you think there will be on the racecourse? Ask children to list everything that will be making a sound.

- **Sports sounds:** Now children should write a list about all the sounds that can be heard on a school sports day. How are the lists different?

Group work

- **Paper, stone scissors:** Introduce the game of paper, stone, scissors. Let children work in pairs to play the game 10 times, recording the winner each time.

- In each group, ask the winner and their partner to talk about how they feel about winning and losing the game.

Drama

- **Role play:** In small groups of three or four, ask children to role play one of the following scenarios with children taking on the different roles. Try to make sure that each scenario, or a variation of it to suit your school, is explored by at least one group.

- After a football match, the team supported by two of the children has won. Those two children can have some kind of celebration, but then what happens in the group?

- One person in the group has been singled out in assembly and given an award for good work in class. How do the others feel, especially those whose work is as good?

- When you have given the groups time to explore their role plays, come back together as a class to discuss the outcomes.

Writing activity

- Complete the speech bubbles on the worksheet to show how the two characters feel.

WINNING AND LOSING

Finish the speech bubbles.

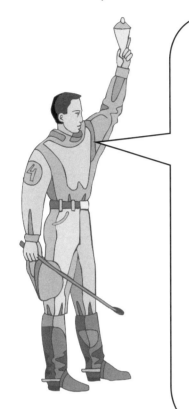

I won! I feel great because

I lost! It wasn't fair because

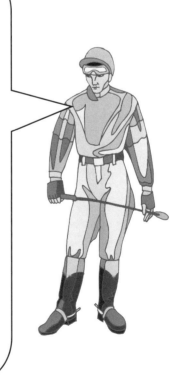

TEACHER'S NOTES

Introduction

- Load up the Mind's Eye CD-ROM. You may like to tell the children what the title of the session is before you reveal the image, or just open up the picture.

- With the image in view, ask the children for their first impressions. What does the picture show? What is happening? Where are these horses and men going?

Familiarisation

- The painting shows the 4th Light Dragoons heading in to battle in the Crimean War. This part of the war was called the Charge of the Light Brigade, when The Light Brigade of the English army galloped against the heavy guns of the Russian army. Most of the English were killed. Those that were wounded, if they were lucky, would have been taken by cart and then shipped to Florence Nightingale's hospital.

Exploration

- Ask the children to look more closely at the image, as if they are detectives, and find out all that they can about it. Is this side winning or losing at the moment? What is the evidence? Why are there so many loose horses? Look at the uniform the men and wearing and their weapons. Would they be useful against cannons? Look at the puffs of smoke coming from the hills in the distance. Can the children guess what they might be? (Cannon fire.)

Lord George Paget leads the 4th Light Dragoons at the Charge of the Light Brigade. © *Mary Evans Picture Library/Alamy*

ACTIVITIES

Speaking

- **Adjectives:** Look at the photograph again. Make a bank of adjectives and adjectival phrases which children can use to describe the conditions shown in the picture. Ask children to use them in the context of a sentence.

- **Empathy:** Continue your list of adjectives, but develop them to include a consideration of how the people and horses are feeling. Again, invite the use of the words and phrases in the context of a sentence. If children have difficulty in framing a sentence, scaffold the construction for them, or model it and ask them to repeat it.

Group work

- **Hopes and fears:** Ask children to imagine being wounded in a battle, like the soldiers in the photograph. What would they be thinking about as they waited to be put into the jolting carts and then into the boats across the Black Sea to hospital in Scutari? What would they be hoping for? What would they fear?

Drama

- **Role play:** Let children work in small groups to role play the experience of being wounded in battle. Where are they wounded? How will that affect how they can move? How will they stand, sit or lie to wait for the carts? Will they talk about reliving the battle? Their families at home? Their hopes and fears for the journey to hospital? Let the groups perform their role play for each other.

Listening

- **Evaluating choices:** As groups watch each others' role plays, encourage the listeners to ask questions about the choices that each of the actors made about their character. Encourage the children to comment on which role plays they liked best and think about ways they could have improved their own group dramas.

Writing activity

- Write a letter home from the perspective of a soldier who was wounded in the Crimean War. The children should use their word banks as well as drawing on the group work and role play activities. Ask them to consider where they would probably be writing from. Would they be in the camp, the cart or the hospital? Will they describe the battle or their journey to the hospital? If you have found out about Florence Nightingale they could include information from those studies to inform their letter. A simple version of this activity could just be to write a letter home from a wounded soldier.

Name _____ Date _____

WOUNDED IN BATTLE

Imagine you are a soldier who has been wounded in battle. Write a letter home to tell your family what has happened and how you are feeling. Don't forget to put a date on your letter.

Date _____

Dear _____

_____

_____

_____

_____

_____

_____

_____

_____

_____

_____

TEACHER'S NOTES

Introduction

• Load up the Mind's Eye CD-ROM. You may like to tell the children what the title of the session is before you reveal the image, or just open up the picture.

• With the image in view, ask the children for their first impressions. What does the picture show? Where is the ladybird? What are the globes below the blade of grass?

Familiarisation

• Check that all children are familiar with ladybirds. Have they ever found any around the school? Outside? Can they tell you where ladybirds live? Where they are likely to be found?

Exploration

• Ask the children to look more closely at the image, as if they are detectives, and find out all that they can about it. How many spots does the ladybird have? (Ladybirds have odd numbers of spots, so it must be a seven-spotted ladybird). Why is the background colour purple, with a darker centre and radiating lines, like the lines on petals? Look carefully at the raindrops hanging from the stalk and see a smaller image of the flower in each one.

• Discuss where the ladybird might be going as it makes its way down the blade of grass. Is its going towards a flower or a leaf? Why is it walking when it could fly?

Seven-spot ladybird (*Coccinella Septempunctata*) on a blade of grass. © *blickwinkel/Alamy*

ACTIVITIES

Speaking

• **Making links:** Ask children what they think the life cycle of a ladybird might be. Those who know the life cycle of a butterfly may be able to recognise the similarity between the insects: the ladybird starts life as a bright yellow egg that hatches in about a week; in its larval stage it looks more like a beetle than a caterpillar, but then it spins a pupa and a week later it emerges as an adult ladybird.

• Once you have shared information about the ladybird's life cycle (www.uksafari.com has lots of child-friendly information), let children draw a chart to show it and then give them the chance to explain how the ladybird develops using their chart and any diagrams as the basis for their presentation.

 Drama

• **Metamorphosis:** Explore how ladybirds move and rest at each stage of the development. Find powerful verbs which describe the movement or state of rest and help children to develop movements which match the verb.

Group work

• **Poem:** Teach the children the old rhyme *Ladybird, ladybird, fly away home/ Your house is on fire and your children are gone.* Let them work in pairs or threes to try to improve on the poem, either with some new lines or with a new poem entirely.

• Let them perform their poems to each other.

Listening

• **Evaluating:** As groups listen to each others' poems, encourage the listeners to ask questions about it. Show the children how to use 'two stars and a wish' (i.e. to say two good things about the poem and one thing that perhaps could have been improved) to give an oral evaluation of the poem.

• The poets should be given the chance to respond to the evaluation and accept what has been suggested, or to justify leaving the poem as it is.

Writing activity

• Use a computer to write up the ladybird poem. Show the children how to 'grab' images from the Internet to illustrate their poem. Ask them to write their poem out on the PCM first.

Name _____   Date _____

A LADYBIRD POEM

Write your ladybird poem here. If you can, find some pictures on the Internet, print them out and stick them on.

Ladybird, ladybird

_____

_____

_____

_____

_____

_____

_____

TEACHER'S NOTES

Introduction

• Load up the Mind's Eye CD-ROM. You may like to tell the children what the title of the session is before you reveal the image, or just open up the picture.

• With the image in view, ask the children for their first impressions. What does the picture show? Is it a real photograph? Why can't it be? (Firstly, where would you stand to take it? And secondly, the planets are too close together and too close to the Sun.)

Familiarisation

• This is a drawing done on a computer to show all of the nine planets. Can the children name any of them? What are the planet's characteristics that enable us to identify them as planets? Name the planets, starting in the bottom left-hand corner, as: Mercury, Venus, Earth, Mars, Jupiter, Saturn, Uranus, Neptune, Pluto.

Exploration

• Ask the children to look more closely at the image, as if they are detectives, and find out all that they can about it. What are the characteristics of each planet that enable us to identify them from picture and photos? Discuss the planets one at a time, considering why it might be difficult for them to sustain life. Consider proximity to the Sun, poisonous atmosphere, lack of water, existence of gases... Talk about the colours chosen to show the planets – which are fairly realistic. What does that tell us about them?

• Look at the image of the Sun. Compare its size to that of the largest planet. Why has the artists chosen those colours to represent the Sun?

Planets of the Solar System. © *ImageState/Alamy*

ACTIVITIES

Speaking

• **Holding conversations:** What do the children think or know about space? Do they know why there isn't any gravity in space? Or that the Moon is in orbit round the Earth due to the Earth's gravity? Or that the planets orbit the Sun due to the Sun's gravity?

• What do children know about the Moon or the stars? Do they think that there is life in space? Can they explain their responses?

Group work

• **Group discussion:** Let children split into small groups to discuss their beliefs about whether or not there is life in space. The group should come to a consensus decision which they all understand. An envoy from each group should be prepared to go into other groups to explain the group's decision and justification.

Drama

• **Exploring space:** Invite the children to make a virtual trip into space with you. Begin by entering the space rocket and counting down from 10. Show how the g-forces affect you during take off, but then relax as you clear the Earth's atmosphere and the friction on the outside of the rocket slows you down.

• When you get far enough into space, open the hatch and go exploring. Don't forget your lifeline giving you air and keeping you attached to the spacecraft. How do you move in space?

Listening

• **Heavenly spheres:** Play the children music that is meant to represent space, such as Holst's Planets Suite, the introduction to Space Odyssey 2001, Star Wars or other music and sound files that you find on the Internet. Ask the children to listen while they are looking at the photograph and then to evaluate the sounds and music.

Writing activity

• Use the PCM to write a space poem. Challenge the children to create it in the shape of a planet.

Name _____ Date _____

SPACE POEM

Write a poem about space in the shape of a planet. Give your poem a title and draw an amazing spaceship at the bottom of the page.

Unit 13/POWER

TEACHER'S NOTES

Introduction

- Load up the Mind's Eye CD-ROM. You may like to tell the children what the title of the session is before you reveal the image, or just open up the picture.

- With the image in view, ask the children for their first impressions. What does the picture show? What time of day is it? Is this picture taken in a city or the countryside? How do you know? (Lines of pylons like this are only usually found crossing the countryside. Also, look at the silhouettes at the foot of the pylons. They're trees, not buildings.)

Familiarisation

- Establish that the function of these pylons is to take electricity safely from place to place.

- Talk about the safety implications of all electricity, but particularly of pylons and generating stations, which have so much electricity.

- Ask the children how much they know about keeping safe around electricity in and out of the home. Discuss some simple safety rules together.

Exploration

- Ask the children to look more closely at the image, as if they are detectives, and find out all that they can about it. How many pylons are there? Are they all of the same design? What do the shapes remind you of? Look at the patterns of shape within each of the pylons.

- Talk about their height compared to the trees growing at their feet. Why is it important that they are so high? What are the problems with building them so high? Look at the sag on the power lines. Why is there so much sag (if possible, link to work on metals contracting at low temperatures)?

Electricity pylons. © *Trevor Smithers ARPS/Alamy*

ACTIVITIES

Speaking

- **Preparing for a debate:** Look at the photograph together. Do children think that, in general, pylons are beautiful, or that they ruin the landscape? Use a toy or a ball for children to pass to each other to allow all of them to express and justify their opinions about pylons.

- Divide the children into three groups, one that think that pylons are beautiful, one that thinks they spoil the landscape and a third who are undecided. Give the children in each group time to talk amongst themselves and to consolidate their opinions

Group work

- **Debate:** Sort the children into groups, each containing one or two children from each of your original three groups. Within the group, the children whose mind is already made up should try to convince the undecided children to adopt their beliefs. At the end of the time, take a straw poll of the children's opinions. Has anyone changed their mind? Why?

Listening

- **Recalling information:** Tell the children that you are going to talk to them about electricity and that you want them to remember three main points you are going to make as well as what the main idea of your talk is.

- Make a short presentation on the use of electricity and electrical equipment and how school would be different without it. Structure it carefully to include the information the children are searching for. Can the children identify your main idea and summarise your main points?

Drama

- **Imagine life without electricity:** Ask children to work in pairs to consider how they would achieve something they need electricity for without electricity. Remind them that batteries store electricity (and that cars need batteries to start) so they have to consider life even without those.

- The children should prepare a short mime, doing something without electricity. Let them perform it for the rest of the class and see if they can work out what the activity is.

Writing activity

- Use the PCM to make a poster about the dangers of electricity for a younger child.

Name _____ Date _____

Make a poster to explain how dangerous electricity is to a younger child.
You can use words and pictures.

DANGER ⚡

TEACHER'S NOTES

Introduction

- Load up the Mind's Eye CD-ROM. You may like to tell the children what the title of the session is before you reveal the image, or just open up the picture.

- With the image in view, ask the children for their first impressions. What do they think the photograph shows? Is this one clock or lots of clocks? How do they know?

Familiarisation

- Can the children read the time on these clocks? Point out that the red tipped hand is the hour hand.

- Can they decide which time shown comes first in the day? (Probably 8 o'clock.) Then which time? Decide which order the clocks should be in if they showed time through the day.

Exploration

- Discuss the fact that the clocks don't show us whether the times are morning or evening. So how do we know which it is?

- Do the children know of any clocks that do tell you whether it's the morning, afternoon or evening?

- Where would you find clocks like the one in the image? Is it an alarm clock? A clock in the town? A church clock? A kitchen clock? A classroom clock? Ask children to explain their response.

Clockfaces showing different times.
© Dynamic Graphics Group/ITStock Free/Alamy

ACTIVITIES

Speaking

- **What's the time?**: Look again at all the times shown on the clocks in the image. Ask children what they think they would be doing at each of the times. Model sequencing two or three of the agreed events into a sequence of sentences, using sequencing words, e.g. *At eight o'clock I have breakfast. After breakfast I get ready for school and I get to school at 9 o'clock. Then we do register and...*

- Can any of the children now make their own sequence of events using sequencing words as you did?

Listening

- **Listen and respond**: Use a tambourine or similar instrument to play slow and loud ticks or quieter rapid ticks. Ask the children to use their bodies to show what kind of clock each sound represents – a big, tall clock or a little curled-up one? Let children take turns in playing the tambourine while the others listen and respond.

Drama

- **What am I doing?**: Model role playing one of the activities you have agreed that you do during the school day. Can the children guess which one you are doing and remember at what time you do it? Let one of them role play a different activity that happens during the school day.

- **Our school day:** Let the children work in small groups to role play a sequence of events during the day. Either each child in the group can choose their own individual role play (e.g. getting up or doing the register) or the group can work together to create the events at each time during the day. Whichever they choose, the outcome should be a short sequence of events they can role play for the rest of the class to watch.

Group work

- **Class game:** Introduce the children to the game of *What's the time Mr Wolf?* Ideally, play it in the hall or outside. One of the children is Mr Wolf and stands against a wall, facing the rest. The others stand at the other end of the space and chant 'What's the time, Mr Wolf?'. Mr Wolf says a time (e.g. *nine o'clock*) and all the children have to take that number of steps forward (e.g. *nine steps*). The game continues until Mr Wolf says 'Dinner time'. At this point she/he has to run and chase all the others back to their starting point. The child who is caught first is the next Mr Wolf.

! Writing activity

- Use the PCM opposite. Children can write or draw to show what they do at certain points in the school day. They can fill in the last clock as they choose to show a different event that happens after school.

WHAT DO YOU DO WHEN?

Look at the times on these clock.
Draw and write what you do at these times.

Draw your own time on this clock and show what you do then.

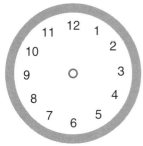

TEACHER'S NOTES

Introduction

• Load up the Mind's Eye CD-ROM. You may like to tell the children what the title of the session is before you reveal the image, or just open up the picture.

• With the image in view, ask the children for their first impressions. What does the picture show? How many whole oranges did the photographer begin with? Why does the whole orange have a leaf on it?

Familiarisation

• Check that children know that oranges grow on trees.

• Can they tell you where in the world oranges grow? How do they get from their trees to us?

Exploration

• Ask the children to look more closely at the image, as if they are detectives, and find out all that they can about it. Look at the texture of the skin. What makes it shiny? Why is it pitted? Consider the skin both on the whole orange and on the parts. Can children see where the skin ends on the cut orange?

• Look carefully at the cut orange pieces. Point out the little sacs that store the juice. Can children see where the orange would divide into segments if it had been peeled rather than cut open?

• Talk about the fractions of orange. The picture shows one whole, one half and two quarters. Do children know how many people could share the oranges if you could see all the halves? (4) And all the quarters? (8)

Oranges shown as whole and cut into half and quarter segments. © *foodfolio/Alamy*

ACTIVITIES

Speaking

• **Descriptions:** Use all the senses to make a thesaurus of words to describe an orange. Think about its taste – juice, flesh and skin, the feel of the skin and of parts of oranges, the smell and what it looks like.

• Introduce the children to similes: *the orange is (smells, tastes, feels, looks) as ___ as a ___. Or the orange smells/ tastes, etc. like a....*

Group work

• **Acrostic:** Let the group work together to make an acrostic of the words and phrases that describe an orange.

Listening

• **Growing oranges:** Tell the children to draw diagrams and pictures to make a flow diagram while you explain all the stages of getting an orange to a table in the UK. There are at least six main points the children will need to sketch while you talk.

• Explain how the orange tree is planted in pre-prepared ground; how it is watered and tended until a flower blooms; how the flower withers and an orange appears. The orange is looked after until it is picked. Then it is loaded into lorries, taken to factories to be sorted and graded, put into crates onto more lorries, then into frozen containers to help to preserve it. More lorries take it to the supermarket, the people in the supermarket unload and unpack it. At last, someone buys it, takes it home and eats it.

• Ask some of the children to use their diagrams and notes to retell the main points of an orange's odyssey.

Drama

• **Mime:** How could we use an orange? Ask children to consider three different things they could do with an orange and to think of a mime to represent each. Do a snowball activity where one child swaps mimes with a partner, then they decide which four mimes are best from their combined repertoire. The pair then joins with another pair and again they perform their mimes. This four then chooses the four best mimes and they join with another four to make an eight. Within the eight, both groups of four perform their four mimes The groups of eight then select four mimes to present to the rest of the class.

Writing activity

• Use the PCM to explore quarters and halves. The children need to work out how many quarters and halves they need to make a fruit salad picture.

Name _____ Date _____

A FRUIT SALAD

How many halves and quarters can you count for each type of fruit? Write the number in the box.

There are ☐ halves of apple.

There are ☐ halves of strawberry.

There are ☐ quarters of banana.

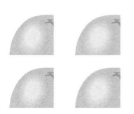

There are ☐ quarters of orange.

Now draw a big picture in the bowl of your fruit salad, making sure you have included all the halves and quarters of fruit you have counted.

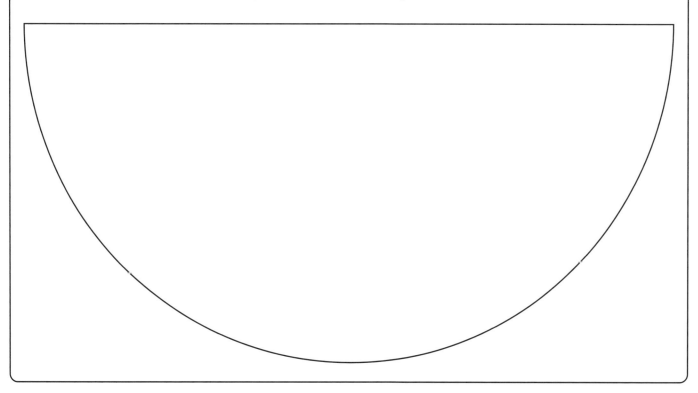

TEACHER'S NOTES

Introduction

• Load up the Mind's Eye CD-ROM. You may like to tell the children what the title of the session is before you reveal the image, or just open up the picture.

• With the image in view, ask the children for their first impressions. What do they think this photograph shows? Where might it have been taken?

Familiarisation

• What do the children know about this dinosaur? It's the head of a Tyrannosaurus rex. Ask different children to add one piece of information each until you have established a class 'fact file' about T. rex.

• Ask the children whether or not they think this is a photograph of a real dinosaur. Clarify that it must be a model. Check that children know that no-one has ever seen a live dinosaur – all that is left are the fossilised bones.

Exploration

• Look at the photograph together and try to find as much information as possible about T. rex. Consider its teeth. What do they tell us about its diet? Look at the bottom teeth. How are they similar to and different from our own?

• What can we tell about the dinosaur's skin? The shape of its head? Whether it looks forwards or out of the side of its head?

• T. rex was believed to be about 12.5 metres long. Relate this to the size of your classroom. If possible, mark out the length on the playground or hall floor.

Tyrannosaurus rex model head.
© Scott Camazine/Alamy

ACTIVITIES

Speaking

• **Images:** Look at the photograph again. Introduce a sentence beginning *It's as scary as...* and ask different children to complete the sentence. Ask children to suggest other sentences beginnings for the images, e.g. *It's as big as...; Its teeth are as sharp as...; Its eyes are as small as...; It runs as fast as...*

• Talk about the different ways children have completed the sentences. What kinds of things did they compare the T. rex to?

Listening

• **Swamp sounds:** Sit quietly in the classroom with the window open and listen to all the sounds you hear around you. Think about what would change if you were in the middle of a prehistoric swamp. What sounds would you hear then?

• Ask different children to try to recreate their idea of one of the swamp sounds. Gradually build up an oral picture of a swamp, with different children making different noises.

Group work

• **Drawing:** Give each group a large piece of paper and ask them to work together to draw and label a swamp.

• The group should nominate one person to describe their swamp to the rest of the class at the end of the session.

Drama

• **T. rex hunt:** Ask the children to stand in a circle while you build a virtual tour of a prehistoric swamp. What will it looks, smell, taste like? What kinds of sounds will you hear?

• Take all the children on a T. rex hunt, following the model of *Going on a Bear Hunt*. Think about the obstacles as you meet them (for example swamp, fallen tree, enormous biting insects, thick undergrowth, long grass, rivers, possibly other dinosaurs) and act out the descriptive verbs to show how you tackle them.

• Once you have finished your T. rex hunt (were you successful?), retell your adventure in the manner of *Going on a Bear Hunt* with refrains to show how the adventure sounded.

Writing activity

• Follow up the drama work with a map of your adventures tracking the T. rex. Ask the children to draw your route, showing all the different kinds of hazards, and labelling them either with the name of the hazard or with the sound you associated with it.

Name _____   Date _____

DINO MAP!

Draw and label a map of your dinosaur hunt. Where did you start and finish?

TEACHER'S NOTES

Introduction

- Load up the Mind's Eye CD-ROM. You may like to tell the children what the title of the session is before you reveal the image, or just open up the picture.

- With the image in view, ask the children for their first impressions. What does the picture show? What is the man doing? What is the pole he is holding in his hand? What is in the fire?

Familiarisation

- The photograph shows a glass blower in Mallorca.

- Have any of the children ever been to a glass blowing factory or seen one on TV? (They are littered around the country in the UK.) If any of the children have, ask them to explain what they saw.

Exploration

- Ask the children to look more closely at the image, as if they are detectives, and find out all that they can about it. Talk about the furnace. Can they see its door is open? Will it always be open? Look at the heart of the fire. It looks white. Do the children know that white heat is hotter than red? Why does a glass blower need such a hot furnace?

- Can the children see any glass anywhere? Establish that the glass is in the furnace to heat it enough to melt and shape it. Link to children's experience with chocolate. When it's hard it's brittle, but if it's allowed to become warm, it softens enough to bend and shape and if it melts completely, it becomes a liquid.

- Explain that the rod in his hand is a steel rod down which the man can blow – like blowing bubbles – or which he can use to twirl the glass. What do the children think the man is making?

Glass-blowing in Mallorca. © *Expuesto-Nicholas Randall/Alamy*

ACTIVITIES

Drama

- **Creating a scene**: take the children into a virtual glass blowing factory. Each of them needs a furnace – with a closed door – and a steel rod.

- Look at the photograph together before you all open the door of the furnace. What does it feel like being hit by the blast of baking air? How do the children react? Stepping back? Covering their eyes from the glare? Bending into the heat?

- Lift up your heavy metal rods and collect a ball of warm glass. Put it into the heart of the furnace to melt it further. Are children going to choose to blow it? It's really hard work, because you have to blow very slowly! Or will they twirl it round to make an interesting shape?

- Continue to work your glass in the fierce heat. Then, when you've finished, shut the furnace door, wipe your face, have a drink and look at what you've made. It's still too hot to pick up, but each of the children should know what they have.

Speaking

- **Glass factory**: Let half of the children wander round the room admiring the glasswork of those who are standing. The wanderers should ask the glass blowers about what they have made, the tricky bits of it, and whether they enjoyed making the object. The glass blowers have the opportunity to show off their creation. Let the groups swap roles.

Listening

- **Remembering**: I went to a glass factory and I saw... ask children to complete the sentence, listing things their friends made in the classroom. Each person can only add one item, but must repeat the list of all the items that have gone before.

Group work

- **Think together**: Let groups of children work together to make a list of everything they can think of that is made of glass or has a glass component. Share the lists and see how many things you have thought of all together.

Writing activity

- Use the PCM to make a flowchart showing how glass is blown. Once the children have completed the drawings on the flowchart, ask them to write brief explanations for each stage.

Name _____ Date _____

HOW TO BLOW GLASS

1

2

3

4

Unit 18/WHOSE STORY?

TEACHER'S NOTES

Introduction

• Load up the Mind's Eye CD-ROM. You may like to tell the children what the title of the session is before you reveal the image, or just open up the picture.

• With the image in view, ask the children for their first impressions. What do they think this painting is about? What time of year is it? How do they know?

Familiarisation

• Introduce the children to the Dutch artist Pieter Bruegel the Elder, who painted scenes of everyday life in some detail. He lived over 300 years ago.

• Ask the children 'What's happening in this picture?' How many different answers can they give you?

Exploration

• Ask the children to look more closely at the image, as if they are detectives, and find out all that they can about it. Look at the individual people and try to work out what they are doing and why.

• Talk about why the artist might have chosen to paint this picture. Do the children think that it's imaginary, or has the artist captured a real event in the days before photography was invented? Discuss the reasons for their answer.

Children playing on the frozen river. Detail from 'The Census of Bethlehem', Pieter Bruegel the Elder. © Muséedes Beaux-Arts, Arras, France/ Giraudon/The Bridgeman Art Library

ACTIVITIES

 Speaking

• **Which picture?**: Look at the photograph again. Begin to create a story about one of the characters. For example, *A man went out to buy some bread for breakfast. The river was frozen and people were skating on it, so he decided to take a short cut across it to get to the bakers. Unfortunately, he stepped on some thin ice, the ice broke under him and he fell through it. The river wasn't too deep, so he didn't drown, but he couldn't get out without help...*

• Can any of the children tell a different story about the man in the ice, or can they tell a story about a different person in the picture?

Group work

• **Sound effects**: Divide the children into small groups. Each group should make up a short story about one of the people and work out how to tell the story complete with sound effects. All of the children should take some part both in the narrative and in the sound effects. Sound effects should include people skating, ice cracking, people laughing and talking, etc.

Drama

• **Role play**: Let the children work in their previous groups. They should now develop their story further by dramatising it. Now, as well as sound effects, they can include dialogue between the different characters in their stories. Remind them that they need to try to maintain the interest of their audience throughout their dramatisation so any details added must strengthen the story, not be a distraction.

Listening

• **Evaluation**: As the children listen to and watch each other's stories and sound effects, ask them to consider what feedback would improve the performance. The feedback should be based on 'Two stars and a wish', i.e. mention two things that were good and one that could be improved.

Writing activity

• Ask children to write the story they have made about the picture. Remind them to use details they managed to include in their dramatisation. In the story, they will also need to create the setting because you can't see the picture in the story.

TELL ME A STORY

A story about Pieter Bruegel's painting.
Give your story a title.

_____

_____

_____

_____

_____

_____

_____

_____

_____

_____

_____

_____

Unit 19/ATTACK!

TEACHER'S NOTES

Introduction

- Load up the Mind's Eye CD-ROM. You may like to tell the children what the title of the session is before you reveal the image, or just open up the picture.

- With the image in view, ask the children for their first impressions. What does the picture show? What are the people doing? Why are they in a cage? What kinds of creatures are near them?

Familiarisation

- Explain the function of a shark cage.

- These sharks are reef sharks, which inhabit many of the coral reefs of the world. They don't usually attack humans unless they feel under threat.

Exploration

- Ask the children to look more closely at the image, as if they are detectives, and find out all that they can about it. How many people are in the cage? Are they men or women? Can you tell? How many sharks are milling around? Are all the fish in the picture sharks?

- Why are there so many bubbles near the top of the picture? Where are they coming from? What equipment are the people wearing? Why do they need any equipment?

- What do the children think the people are *doing* in the cage? Is this something they would choose to do, or is it some kind of punishment? Why would people choose to go into shark-infested waters? And why would they go in a cage?

- Is the cage near to the sea bed? Where is the evidence needed to answer that question?

Schooling reef sharks surround a suspended shark cage containing scuba divers. © *Stephen Frink Collection/Alamy*

ACTIVITIES

 Drama

- **Create a setting:** Take the children into the cage, under the sea. What are they wearing? Remind them to breathe slowly through their mouths. Remind them too that they cannot speak, so need to communicate by gesture or with their eyes. How do they move under water? Can they move quickly or slowly? What does the water feel like as it flows past their faces and over their bodies? What can they see?

- Let them become the sea creatures around them: *there are sharks and smaller, quicker moving fish; on the sea bed there will be crabs and sea anemones waving their tentacles. What else?*

Speaking

- **Begin a story:** Look at the photograph together to begin your story. Are you going to tell the story from the point of view of the people in the cage, the sharks or the people in the boat above the cage?

- Having decided on the point of view character, begin to ask the children questions to scaffold the beginning of the story: *How did the people get there? Why did they get there? How do they feel about being there? How do the sharks feel about them being there? What are the possible problems or dangers that might lead to the story becoming interesting? Are the people going to open the cage door? Is the cage going to drop to the sea bed? Are the sharks going to attack the cage?*

Group work

- **Continue the story:** The children can work in pairs to continue the story from the point at which the class story stopped. *What exciting action is going to come from the problem you identified? How will the problem be solved and the story end?* The children should tell their whole story to their partner.

Listening

- **Evaluating the story:** Ask the children to swap partners and each should tell their story to their new partner. The new partners should repeat the highlights of the story and evaluate with two stars and a wish (two good things and something that could be improved).

Writing activity

- Write up the story on the PCM and draw a scary shark to illustrate it.

Name _____   Date _____

UNDER THE SEA

Write your shark story here. Give your story a title and draw your own scary shark in the bubble!

_____

_____

_____

_____

_____

_____

_____

_____

TEACHER'S NOTES

Introduction

• Load up the Mind's Eye CD-ROM. You may like to tell the children what the title of the session is before you reveal the image, or just open up the picture.

• With the image in view, ask the children for their first impressions. What does the picture show? What is the man doing? What kind of work does he do? How can you tell?

Familiarisation

• The man is a pizza chef. When pizza dough is nearly ready to cook it is very stretchy. The chef kneads it until he's satisfied with it, then he pushes it into shape with his fingers. But to get that thin, crispy pizza base, he throws the disc of dough into the air to let it widen naturally and evenly without the risk of putting his fingers through the thinning dough.

Exploration

• Ask the children to look more closely at the image, as if they are detectives, and find out all that they can about it. Why is there still a lump of dough left on the counter? What's it for? What's on the counter beside the lump of dough? Why does he need two different kinds of cheese?

• Look at the machines behind the chef. What are they for? Can they see the cups to put the coffee into once it's made? What are all the plates behind him for? What are all the bottles on the wall? Why might he need them?

Pizza chef thowing a dough base.
© *Vladimir Godnik/Alamy*

ACTIVITIES

Listening

• **Remembering the main points:** Tell the children that you're going to tell them how to make a pizza. At the end, you want them to be able to remember the four main stages.

  • Explain how the dough is made from water, flour, salt and yeast. It's then left to rise and put in a fridge overnight.

  • The dough is taken out of the fridge and kneaded, pushed out into shape. Some chefs then throw it in the air to make in thin and crispy.

  • The topping is put on the pizza. This usually has a base of tomato sauce, then some sliced meats or vegetables and at least one kind of cheese.

  • When the pizza is ready it is put in a very hot oven for a short period of time.

Speaking

• **Giving instructions:** Ask all the children to tell a partner how to make a pizza. They should include the four main stages: making the dough, shaping the dough, adding the topping, cooking.

Drama

• **Making a pizza:** Let the children work in groups of four to mime making a pizza. The first child should make and knead the dough, the second should push it out and throw it in the air, the third should add the toppings and the fourth should cook the pizza. All the children should have a turn at all the roles.

• When all the 'pizzas' are made, ask the children to take their pizzas around the room and try to 'sell' their slices to each other. The pizza maker should tell the customer what the toppings are and whether or not they've made a very thin base. The pizza maker needs to make it sound sufficiently appetising that the customer wants to try a slice.

Group work

• **Giving and following instructions:** Let the children work in pairs. One should give instructions for making a pizza and the other should do exactly what they're told. If the instructions are not clear, the do-er should ask for clarification.

Writing activity

• Use the PCM to write up a recipe for making pizza. Get the children to list their favourite toppings and make up a name for their pizza recipe.

Name _____ Date _____

PIZZA RECIPE

Write your recipe for making a pizza here.

What you need:

_____ _____

_____ _____

_____ _____

What to do:

_____

_____

_____

_____

_____

My favourite pizza toppings are:

_____ _____

_____ _____

On the menu, this pizza is called

_____

TEACHER'S NOTES

Introduction

• Play the first few seconds of the audio clip, then pause it. Invite the children to suggest what could be making this sound.

• Continue to play the whole clip to the class. Discuss the children's first impressions and invite them to say what kind of machine could be making the noise

Familiarisation

• Replay the clip. Establish that it's an aeroplane taking off.

• Have any of the children ever been in an aeroplane? Ask them to share their experiences of taking off. Were they frightened? Were they excited? What kind of noise did they hear?

Exploration

• Listen to the clip again while you ask the children to think about all the information they can get from it. Was the clip recorded from inside the plane or from outside? Help children to recognise that it might be from outside because we can hear the sounds of the plane approaching then disappearing.

• Ask the children to shut their eyes and listen. They should put their hands up when the sound of the aeroplane engine has disappeared into the distance.

• Does the aircraft engine sound change or just get closer and further away? Why is this?

Audio clip
PASSENGER JET (51 secs)

ACTIVITIES

Speaking:

• **Discussion:** Why do people go on aeroplanes? Think of as many reasons as possible, e.g. holidays, for business, to see friends and family, because they work on the plane, to travel, to go and live in a new country, to accompany things from one country to another, for military purposes. Ask those children who have been on a plane why they went on a plane.

• **Planning a holiday:** Ask the children where they would like to go for their holiday destination. What do they want to do when they get there? Use democratic voting to agree on one destination.

Drama

• **Going on holiday:** Organise the children so that they are seated in twos and threes, as on a plane. Make sure they fasten their seatbelts. Warn them when the plane is going to start its take-off and as it taxies down the runway, do the safety announcements such as where the exit doors are, the existence of little lights in case of emergency to light-up the route to the exit doors, where to find the life raft etc.

• Sit down for take-off and ask the children to sit back in their seats while the plane takes off and gains height.

• Once the plane is airborne, ask the children what they expect to see and feel (both emotionally and in terms of temperature) as the plane touches down. Make sure everyone is strapped in again and leaning back in their seats for the landing.

Group work

• **Exploring a destination:** Let the children work in small groups. Ask them to leave the plane together and to explore their destination (away from the airport). They might choose to look at their hotel accommodation first, or check out the swimming pool or the beach (depending on your destination).

• What was it that drew you to this destination? Make sure that the children explore and discuss all of the possibilities.

Listening

• **Holding a conversation:** Let children walk round the room, meeting and greeting old friends, asking about their holidays, talking about their own experiences and asking each other questions.

Writing activity

• Use the PCM to write up a diary of a real or imaginary holiday. Children should decide where their holiday takes place, what sort of activities there are, and who they are on holiday with. Remind them about the features of diaries.

Name _____ Date _____

HOLIDAY DIARY

Write a diary entry describing your favourite holiday.
It can be a real or made-up holiday

Day 1 _____

_____

_____

_____

_____

Day 2 _____

_____

_____

_____

_____

Day 3 _____

_____

_____

_____

_____

Unit 22/WHICH ANIMAL?

TEACHER'S NOTES

Introduction

- Play the first few seconds of the audio clip, then pause it. Have any of the children listened to music like this before?

- Continue to play the whole clip to the class. Discuss the children's first impressions and invite them to say what kind of music they are listening to. How many people are playing instruments? (A symphony orchestra.)

Familiarisation

- Replay the clip. Tell children that this music is intended to represent an animal. Can they guess which animal it is? What clues can they use?

- Listen one more time to the audio clip. It's from Prokofiev's *Peter and the Wolf*. Give the children options of the characters in the story: Peter, Grandpa, a wolf, a cat, a duck, a bird and hunters.

Exploration

- Listen to the clip again while you ask the children to think about all the information they can get from it. Listen first to the orchestra. Do any of the children recognise the sound of the instrument that represents the cat? It's a clarinet.

- Let the children move to the music. Is this a running cat, a sleeping cat or a walking cat? How can they tell? Does the cat ever stretch out, or purr?

Audio clip
'Cat' from *PETER AND THE WOLF*, Prokofiev (51 secs)

ACTIVITIES

Drama

- **Exploration:** How do different animals move? Talk about what makes the difference between animals in terms of their movements.

- Let different children choose an animal and move round the room being their animal. When you clap your hands they should move to the nearest person and see if they can guess each others' animal.

- When the children move on, they should adopt a different animal persona.

Speaking

- **Who am I?:** Moving is one way of describing an animal, but there are others. What other characteristics would you use when you describe an animal? For example, size, colour, hair or fur, noises, habitat, strengths, weaknesses, special characteristics.

- Ask each child to think of an animal description. What clues would they give someone about their animal if they wanted the person to guess it quickly? How about if they wanted the person to have to work hard at guessing?

- Let some of the children give their clues to the others. How fluently can they present their information?

Group work

- **Preparing questions and answers:** Introduce the game '20 Questions', explaining the rules. Focus particularly on the fact that the questions can only be answered with the words 'yes' or 'no'.

- Let the children work in small groups. Within the group, they should consolidate the information they know about three animals in preparation to being asked questions. They will at least need to know at least the answers to the information you discussed earlier.

Listening

- **20 questions:** Let children work in pairs, when both children come from different groups. Within the pair, both children should try to guess the creature. Remind the questioner to think about information they have already gained before asking their next question.

- Once both children have found the creature, let the children work in a different pair.

Writing activity

- Use the PCM to write clues about a creature for others to read and guess what the creature is. They can also draw or stick in a 'picture clue'.

Name _____ Date _____

WHO AM I?

Read the clues and guess the animal.

Clue 1 _____

Clue 2 _____

Clue 3 _____

Clue 4 _____

Clue 5 _____

Clue 6 _____

Clue 7 _____

Clue 8 _____

Clue 9 _____

Clue 10

PICTURE CLUE

ANSWER: I am a _____

Unit 23/GOOD OR BAD?

TEACHER'S NOTES

Introduction

• Play the first few seconds of the audio clip, then pause it. Invite the children to suggest what could be making this sound.

• Continue to play the whole clip to the class. Discuss the children's first impressions and invite them to say what kind of animals they are listening to. How do they know? What are the clues that distinguish this animal from similar animals?

Familiarisation

• Replay the clip. This is a pack of wolves.

• What do the children know about wolves? Which countries do they live in? (Cold countries like Siberia.) Do they live in groups, or alone? (In packs.) What do they eat? (Meat.)

Exploration

• Listen to the clip again while you ask the children to think about all the information they can get from it. Is this one wolf or a pack of wolves?

• What do the children think the wolves are communicating? Are they happy, angry, frightened, worried? What are the signs that the children can identify to justify their answers?

Audio clip
WOLVES (55 secs)

ACTIVITIES

Speaking:

• **Wolves in stories:** Which traditional tales can the children think of that contain wolves as one of the main characters? (*Three Little Pigs, Little Red Riding Hood*). What kind of character is the wolf in those stories?

• Discuss why the wolf might be portrayed as a bad character in these stories. Are there any stories in which the wolf is a good character?

🎭 Drama:

• **Good and bad characters:** How do wolves move? Ask the children to try to create the walk and look of a wicked, scheming wolf. Then of a happy, kindly wolf. What has changed about the way they move and look around themselves?

• Explore how other characters in traditional tales might change from good to bad. Think about characters like the Billy Goats Gruff. How would they walk as their usual characters in the story? How would that change if they were scheming to steal the fresh green grass from the good-tempered troll? How would the troll change? In Sleeping Beauty, both the princess and the prince are good characters and the thirteenth fairy is the wicked one. How would the characters look and move differently if they were swapped over? Talk about how baddies are portrayed in traditional tales.

👁 Group work

• **Retelling a story with a twist:** Let children work in small groups. Within their group, they should agree on a traditional tale they would like to retell – but this time they must swap over two characters, so a good character becomes bad and a bad character becomes good.

• Let the children use dramatic techniques as well as just discussing how their new story would develop. Does it need to change with the characters? How will they show their audience that the characters have changed?

👂 Listening

• **Evaluating:** Let each group tell and perform its story with a twist to another group. The listening children should focus on how the group has swapped the characteristics of two of the characters and how well the storytellers have adapted the story.

• The listeners should each make two comments on the story, at least one of which has to be positive and different from what has previously been said.

❗ Writing activity

• On the PCM the children should write a list of good and bad characteristics for two of their favourite fairytale characters. They can make up what they think would make them good or bad, depending on whether they start off as heroes or villains.

Name _____   Date _____

HERO OR VILLAIN?

Write down the names of your two favourite fairytale characters. For each one, write a list of things that make them good, then a list of things that could make them bad. If they are already bad, make up some things that might be nice about them!

Character 1 _____

GOOD	BAD

Character 2 _____

GOOD	BAD

Unit 24/MAKING COSTUMES

TEACHER'S NOTES

Introduction

- Play the first few seconds of the audio clip, then pause it. Invite the children to suggest what could be making this sound.

- Continue to play the whole clip to the class. Discuss the children's first impressions and invite them to say what they think they are listening to. What are the clues that tell them the answer?

Familiarisation

- Replay the clip. The sound is of scissors cutting fabric.

- Can the children suggest different reasons why someone might want to cut fabric? For example: for collage and decorative work; to make clothes, to make costumes for plays, to make toys, for upholstery – making seat covers or cushions, to make curtains.

- Have any of the children ever cut fabric? How is it different from cutting paper?

Exploration

- Listen to the clip again while you ask the children to think about all the information they can get from it. How many pairs of scissors are in the recording? Is the fabric being cut thick or thin? How could you tell? Are the scissors cutting in a straight line? What is the evidence?

- What do the children think this person might be cutting out? How can they guess from the audio clip alone?

Audio clip
SCISSORS CUTTING FABRIC (22 secs)

ACTIVITIES

Group work

- **Designing a costume:** Let children work in groups of about three. Each group will need a large sheet of paper and a marker pen. Within each group the children should identify a character from a traditional tale they know and they should plan the costume that one of them would wear if the class performed that traditional tale.

- The children should draw and label the costume.

Speaking

- **Explaining:** Each group should send an envoy into a new group to explain the design of the costume. They should refer to the diagram while they speak so that their presentation is a mixture of speech and gesture. If possible, allow all of the children in a group to explain their costume design to a different group.

Listening

- **Making suggestions:** The listening group should comment on the design and make suggestions for improvements. Encourage them to ask questions that challenge the ideas behind the decisions without belittling them.

- The envoys should then return to their group and pass on the suggestions for improvements, which should be discussed and either implemented or rejected. Another envoy could take the improved design to a new group and repeat the process.

Drama

- **Presenting a story:** Put the children in different groups, and allocate a traditional story to each of the groups. Make sure that the group has the correct number of characters for the story.

- Give the children time to allocate parts in the play, then ask them to improvise dialogue to retell the story – without a narrator to hold the story together.

Writing activity

- Use the PCM to show the design of their costume. The children should draw the costume in the space provided and write labels where appropriate. Remind them that the costume should be for a specific character. What is the fabric like? Is it tough, thin, furry or smooth? Is it plain or patterned? What colours will they use? Does the character need to be very active and will this affect the costume? At the foot of the sheet they should write a short explanation of the choices they made.

Name _____ Date _____

MAKING COSTUMES

A costume for _____

in the story of _____

Draw the costume in the box. Add labels to help explain your design.
Then write about your costume at the bottom of the page.

_____

_____

_____

Unit 25/IN THE PLAYGROUND

TEACHER'S NOTES

Introduction

• Play the first few seconds of the audio clip, then pause it. Invite the children to suggest what could be making this sound.

• Continue to play the whole clip to the class. Discuss the children's first impressions and invite them to say what they think they are listening to. Do any of the children know this song?

Familiarisation

• Replay the clip. The song is 'Here we go Looby Loo'.

• What do the children know about this song? Is it a quiet song? Where might they sing songs like this? At parties? At school? In the playground?

• What other songs and playground games do the children enjoy?

Exploration

• Listen to the clip again while you ask the children to think about all the information they can get from it. How many children do they think are singing? How old are the children? Are they trained singers or just a group of ordinary children?

• Ask the children where they think the children on the audio clip are. There's no music track or piano playing. Does this affect the answer?

Audio clip
HERE WE GO LOOBY LOO (1 min 24 secs)

ACTIVITIES

 Drama

• **Sing the song and play the game:** Let all of the children join in while you sing the song together in a circle and do all of the actions. If you don't know the song well enough, follow it on the audio clip.

• What other playground songs and games do the children know that work in a circle? Maybe they know *I sent a letter to my love and on the way I dropped it. In and out the dusty bluebells. Musical chairs.*

• Play some circle time games, for example, Fruit Salad. Give each child the name of one of six pieces of fruit. Have a name yourself. Call out two pieces of fruit. The children with that name have to stand up and swap seats with someone else who is standing up. Ring the changes by calling out three pieces of fruit or even 'fruit salad' where everyone has to swap places. Add another dimension to the game by sitting the children on chairs and making sure that there is one fewer chair than there are people (the caller stays standing). The last person to swap seats has to stand in the middle and call out the next two pieces of fruit.

Group work

• **Inventing a new game:** Each group should try to invent a new playground game. It can be based on an existing one (i.e. it could be a variation of 'tag' or 'hopscotch', or could even be based on a song), but with a new twist, or it could be an entirely new game. You may want to tell the children if there is equipment they can use.

Speaking

• **Explaining the game:** Ask one child from a group to give the rest of the class instructions as to how to play the game his or her group has just invented. Remind the speaker to be specific and clear because all the others will not know how to play the game.

Listening

• **Asking questions:** The children who are listening should try to clarify any misunderstandings before they get up and try to play the new game. Encourage them to 'see' the instructions inside their heads. If they can't, or they don't know what's going on, they will need to ask questions to ensure that they all know what to do.

• Give the children a short time to try out the new game. If possible, allow more children to explain their game to at least another group of children.

Writing activity

• Use the PCM to write instructions for their game. Remind them of the need for clarity and precision. Try to encourage them to write their instructions within five steps.

Name _____   Date _____

RULES OF THE GAME

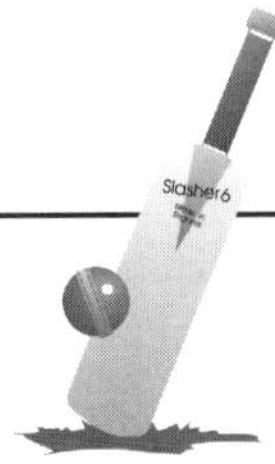

Draw or write in the boxes to explain the rules of the game
you made up in your lesson.

Instructions for the game of _____

Equipment needed: _____

1

2

3

4

5

Unit 26/HOUSE AND GARDEN

TEACHER'S NOTES

Introduction

- This is a task that involves finishing a picture according to given instructions. The task is not intended to encourage creativity, but listening skills. The quality of the resulting picture is not an issue, as long as the instructions have been followed correctly. A printable PDF of the script is on the CD-ROM.

- There is a short pause at the end of each instruction to indicate that the instruction has finished. You will need to pause the CD at these points in order to give your children the time they will need to complete each task.

- Each of the children will need:
  - a pencil and
  - a copy of the worksheet.

- Explain to the children that their task is to:
  - Listen to the instructions on the CD-ROM.
  - Wait until the end of each instruction, then do as it asks. All of the instructions involve drawing or writing.

Instructions on CD
(5 mins 03 secs)

ACTIVITIES

Speaking

- **Finish it:** Give each of the children another copy of the worksheet and a pencil. Let each of the children in turn say aloud their own instruction to finish the picture. You may need to model giving clear instructions first. Encourage children to ask questions if they need to clarify, for example, the position, size or orientation of anything they are told to draw.

 Group work

- **Giving instructions:** Divide the children into groups of four or five. Within each group, the children should further subdivide into pairs or threes.

- Each group needs to collect ten different items from around the classroom, for example cubes, shapes, construction blocks, counting apparatus, small toys. The items must all have a duplicate so that each team of two or three children has exactly the same items. Each team will also need a large book or other barrier and a sheet of A4 paper with L and R written in the top corners to indicate left and right.

- With the barrier up between them, one of the teams should give the other instructions to arrange the 10 items in a certain pattern on the A4 paper. Encourage the use of precise instructions, but also the need for the listening team to ask for clarification if the instructions aren't clear enough.

 Drama

- **Freeze-frame:** Ask the children to think of a story you have read recently.

- Divide them into small groups, each of which has sufficient children to represent all of the characters in the story plus one other.

- Each group needs to nominate a director. The director needs to give each of the others instructions to make a freeze-frame of part of the story you have agreed upon. The director cannot touch any other child or demonstrate what she wants them to do – the instructions can only be spoken.

🛈 Writing activity

- Let children work in groups to make poster plans of the school. Each of the children within the group should decide for themselves where in the school they would hide 'treasure'! They should write clear instructions to tell other children how to reach the treasure, starting from your classroom.

Name _____   Date _____

HOUSE AND GARDEN

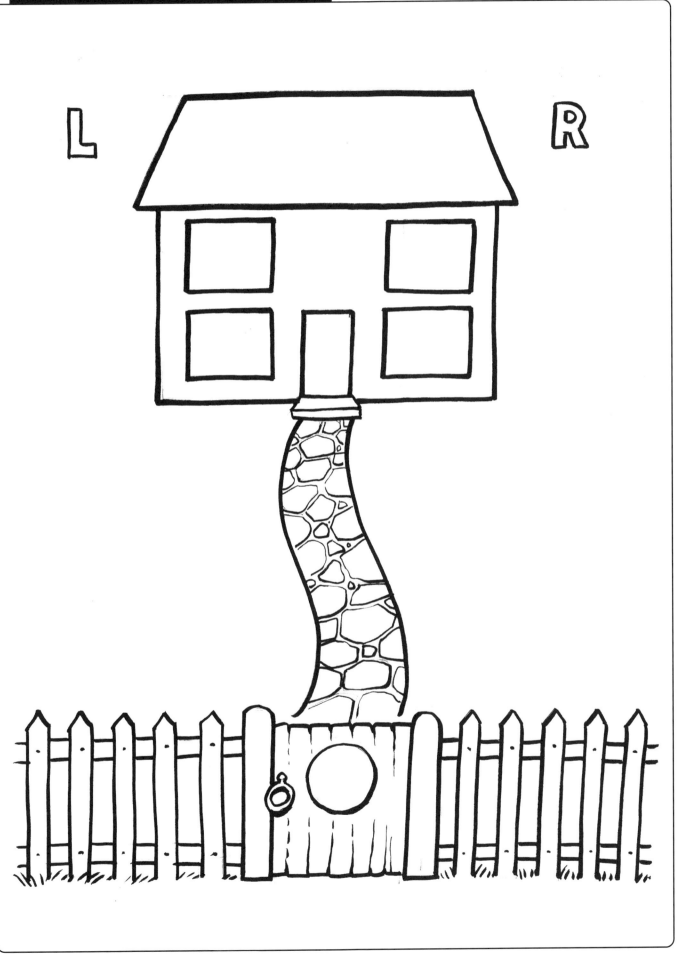

Mind's Eye Y2/Speaking & Listening   Unit 26/HOUSE AND GARDEN

TEACHER'S NOTES

Introduction

- This is a task that involves finishing a picture according to given instructions. The task is not intended to encourage creativity, but listening skills. The quality of the resulting picture is not an issue, as long as the instructions have been followed correctly. A printable PDF of the script is on the CD-ROM.

- There is a short pause at the end of each instruction to indicate that the instruction has finished. You will need to pause the CD at these points in order to give your children the time they will need to complete each task.

- Each of the children will need:
  - a writing pencil,
  - red, blue and green colouring pencils and
  - a copy of the worksheet.

- Explain to the children that their task is to:
  - Listen to the instructions on the CD-ROM.
  - Wait until the end of each instruction, then do as it asks. All of the instructions involve drawing or writing.

Instructions on CD
(4 mins 01 secs)

ACTIVITIES

Speaking

- **Get in line:** Ask some of the children to make a line, but nominate them according to what they are wearing or what they look like rather than by their names. Don't let them make a line according to the order in which you call them out, but use ordinal numbers and positioning words. Give them additional instructions about how to stand, e.g. *face the back of the queue and put one arm in the air.*

- Let some of the children give instructions for others to make a line. They should follow your model when they make a line. Encourage those who are making a line to ask questions in order to clarify position, etc.

Group work

- **Finish it:** The children should work in pairs. Give each of them a blank piece of paper and some coloured pencils. They will also need a large book as a barrier.

- One of the children should give instructions to their partner on how to draw one or more characters on the paper. Encourage children to ask questions if they need to clarify, for example, the position, size or orientation of anything they are told to draw.

Drama

- **How do you feel?:** Let children work in groups. Within each group, each child needs to decide on an emotion they want to express then stand or sit in such a way that his/her feelings are clear to the others. Other children in the group should try to identify the emotion being expressed and to describe how they know. They can use their faces or body language, but must mime throughout.

Writing activity

- Ask each child to write some instructions about drawing five people standing in a line. Remind children to include information about: whether each person is male or female, an adult, child or baby, what colour skin and hair they have, what they are wearing, if they are carrying anything and what their expression is like. They should swap their instructions with a partner, then each should draw according to the others' instructions.

BUS STOP

TEACHER'S NOTES

Introduction

- This is a task that involves finishing a picture according to given instructions. The task is not intended to encourage creativity, but listening skills. The quality of the resulting picture is not an issue, as long as the instructions have been followed correctly. A printable PDF of the script is on the CD-ROM.

- There is a short pause at the end of each instruction to indicate that the instruction has finished. You will need to pause the CD at these points in order to give your children the time they will need to complete each task.

- Each of the children will need:
  - a pencil and
  - a copy of the worksheet.

- Explain to the children that their task is to:
  - Listen to the instructions on the CD-ROM.
  - Wait until the end of each instruction, then do as it asks. All of the instructions involve drawing or writing.

Instructions on CD
(4 mins 04 secs)

ACTIVITIES

Speaking

- **Finish it:** Give each of the children another copy of the worksheet and a pencil. Let each of the children in turn say aloud their own instruction to finish the picture. You may need to model giving clear instructions first. Encourage children to ask questions if they need to clarify, for example, the position, size or orientation of anything they are told to draw.

Group work

- **Giving instructions:** Divide the children into groups of four or five. Within each group, the children should further subdivide into pairs or threes. Each pair or three needs a piece of paper with three lines drawn across it for shelves.

- With the barrier up between them, one of the teams should give the other instructions to draw 10 mugs on the lines. Encourage the use of precise instructions, but also the need for the listening team to ask for clarification if the instructions aren't clear enough.

Drama

- **Nice cuppa?:** The children can work in small groups. At any given time, one child will be role playing while the others in the group watch.

- The child who is role playing should first make themselves a drink, miming opening tins or packets, finding what they need and putting it into the mug, pouring in liquid, stirring if necessary and then drinking. They will need to decide whether or not they like the drink or dislike it, whether it's too hot or too cold. All of this, they should communicate through mime. The audience in each group need to guess what's in the mug.

ⓘ Writing activity

- Children can write instructions for making their favourite drink. Remind them of the key features of instruction writing, including: beginning with a goal, listing ingredients, separating each instruction and using 'command' verbs. They could also keep a tally chart of how many drinks they have during the day and add them up over a whole week.

Name _____ Date _____

DESIGN A MUG COMPETITION

TEACHER'S NOTES

Introduction

• This is a task that involves following a route according to given instructions. The quality of the outcome is not an issue, as long as the instructions have been followed correctly. A printable PDF of the script is on the CD-ROM.

• There is a short pause at the end of each instruction to indicate that the instruction has finished. You will need to pause the CD at these points in order to give your children the time they will need to complete each task.

• Each of the children will need:
  • a pencil and
  • a copy of the worksheet.

• Explain to the children that their task is to:
  • Listen to the instructions on the CD-ROM.
  • Wait until the end of each instruction, then do as it asks. All of the instructions involve drawing or writing.

Instructions on CD
(5 mins 02 secs)

ACTIVITIES

Speaking

• **Finish it:** Give each of the children another copy of the worksheet and a pencil. Let each of the children in turn say aloud their own instructions for the mouse to get through the maze. You may need to model giving clear instructions first. Encourage children to ask questions if they need to clarify, for example, the position, or size of anything they are told to draw.

 Group work

• **Maze story:** In small groups, ask children to invent their own maze story. They should decide who is trying to get to the centre of the maze, why, and the dangers they will face when they get it wrong. When they have agreed their story, ask the children to draw it on a piece of paper.

• Each group should then nominate one of their members to go and explain the story to a different group.

 Drama

• **Robotics:** Let the children work in pairs. One of them should be a robot, moving according to the instructions of the other. The child giving the instructions needs to tell the robot when to walk, how many steps to take, when and where to turn, etc.

• Can the child giving instructions each time get the 'robot' to walk in a square? Or a rectangle? Or spell a letter of the alphabet? Or make a number like you see on calculators?

Writing activity

• Children can write and draw their own maze story. First, they should draw their maze. What kind of creatures or characters will they put in their mazes? Where will they hide the characters? What prize will be in the middle of the maze? Give the children the opportunity to listen to the CD again so that they can hear the language which is appropriate for this kind of story.

CAT AND MOUSE

START

Unit 30/CHIME BARS

TEACHER'S NOTES

Introduction

• This is a task that involves writing a tune according to given instructions. The task is designed to encourage children to distinguish high and low notes as they develop their listening skills. The final outcome will be notation showing a short tune on two chime bars. A printable PDF of the script is on the CD-ROM.

• There is a short pause at the end of each instruction to indicate that the instruction has finished. You will need to pause the CD at these points in order to give your children the time they will need to complete each task.

• Each of the children will need:
  • a pencil and
  • a copy of the worksheet.

• Explain to the children that their task is to:
  • Listen to the instructions on the CD-ROM.
  • Wait until the end of each instruction, then write the letters that represent the sounds. All of the instructions involve writing the letter C or c.

Instructions on CD
(4 mins 12 secs)

ACTIVITIES

Speaking

• **Musical instruments**: Get a selection of percussion instruments. Play them to children and ask children to think of words to describe the sound each one makes.

• Ask children to shut their eyes. Play one of the instruments again. Ask children both to identify the instrument and to describe how they knew which instrument it was. Don't accept *I just did*, but probe more deeply to elicit descriptions of the sound they heard and how it was different from other sounds.

Group work

• **Composition**: Divide the children into groups of six or seven and give each group a selection of three or four percussion instruments. Half of the children should choose an instrument and then co-operate to compose a short piece of music in which each person plays two notes on their instrument – not necessarily both together.

• When the tune has been played through twice, the instruments should swap hands and those who were listening should try to repeat the tune from memory. Different children should then become composers.

Drama

• Divide the children into groups of seven or eight. Within each group, the children should take turns to be the composer. The composer's job is to organise the others to stand high or low. As each child is put in position, they should sing their note, high if they are standing straight or low if they are crouching down.

• Once all the children are in position, the composer should become the conductor, pointing to each child in turn so that they sing their note. The composer can point to different children for different lengths of time in order to bring a rhythm into their composition. All of the children should have a chance to be the composer/ conductor.

🔊 Writing activity

• Put out a section of musical instruments. Children can fold a piece of paper in half like a card. On the outside, they should write a description of one of the instruments, including describing what it looks like and the sound it makes. Inside the 'card' they should draw the instrument and write its name. They can share their descriptions with each other and see if the listener can guess which instrument is being described.

CHIME BARS

OPPORTUNITIES FOR CROSS-CURRICULAR LINKS TO QCA SCHEMES OF WORK (DfES Standards Site) in Mind's Eye Y2

	IMAGES Mind's Eye Y2 Units	Cross-curricular links (QCA Schemes of work)
1	TELL ME A STORY	**D&T:** Unit 2B Puppets
2	NATURE ALL AROUND	**Art:** Unit 2B Mother Nature, designer
3	BUILDING SHAPES	**Art:** Unit 2C Can buildings speak?
4	WHOSE CAR?	**D&T:** Unit 2A Vehicles
5	GOAL	**PE:** Unit 4 Games activities
6	FOOTPRINTS IN THE SAND	**Geography:** Unit 3 An island home
7	THOSE WERE THE DAYS	**History:** Unit 3 What were seaside holidays like in the past?
8	ISLAND HOME	**Geography:** Unit 3 An island home
9	SPORT OF KINGS	**History:** Unit 5 How do we know about the Great Fire of London?
10	WAR!	**History:** Unit 4 Why do we remember Florence Nightingale?
11	LADYBIRDS	**Science:** Unit 2B Plants and animals in the local environment
12	HEAVENLY SPHERES	**Science:** Unit 2E Forces and movement
13	POWER	**Science:** Unit 2F Using electricity
14	WHEN DO WE?	**Numeracy:** Understand and use the vocabulary related to time; Read the time to the half or quarter hour on analogue clocks
15	HOW MUCH IS MINE?	**Maths:** Understand and use fractions: part, one whole, one half, one quarter
16	DINOSAUR HUNT	**Literacy:** Reading and talking
17	BLOWING GLASS	**Literacy:** Speaking and listening
18	WHOSE STORY?	**Art:** Unit 2A Picture this! Picture this!
19	ATTACK!	**Literacy:** Speaking and listening
20	WHAT'S FOR DINNER?	**Literacy:** Speaking and listening

	SOUNDS Mind's Eye Y2 Units	Cross-curricular links (QCA Schemes of work)
21	WE'RE OFF	**Literacy:** Speaking and listening
22	WHICH ANIMAL?	**Literacy:** Speaking and listening
23	GOOD OR BAD?	**Literacy:** Traditional tales
24	MAKING COSTUMES	**Literacy:** Traditional tales
25	IN THE PLAYGROUND	**Literacy:** Traditional tales
26	HOUSE AND GARDEN	**Art:** Unit 2C Can buildings speak?
27	BUS STOP	**Literacy:** Speaking and listening
28	MUGS FOR SALE	**Literacy:** Speaking and listening
29	CAT AND MOUSE	**ICT:** Unit 2D Controlling a floor turtle
30	CHIME BARS	**Music:** Unit 1 Section 7 Listening, memory and movement